AF557803

Praise for the Book

Journeys to Nirvana is a testament to travel as transformation, an inner awakening as much as a worldly adventure. With evocative prose and striking images drawn from years spent moving through landscapes and lives, Vivek Bammi offers more than a visual diary; he presents a worldview shaped by movement, mindfulness, and meaning. Through his lens, nirvana reveals itself not only as spiritual fulfilment, but as liberation—from habit, from prejudice, and the quiet prisons of cultural conditioning.

Rooted in formative years spent amidst the wild beauty of Assam, Bammi's lifelong wanderlust finds its voice in journeys that are both outward and inward. Echoing Lord Indra's timeless wisdom that the wandering soul grows and bears fruit like the blossoming flower, Bammi explores how nature, solitude, impermanence, and exchange reveal the deeper structures of perception and belonging. As someone who has long believed in the power of travel to dismantle prejudice and broaden the mind, I found in these pages a kindred spirit. *Journeys to Nirvana* also invites a return to curiosity; to see in difference not a threat but an opportunity for mutual recognition and understanding. Bammi's meditative reflections and richly human encounters compel us to step beyond the confines of constructed identities and embrace the world in all its multiplicity.

—Shashi Tharoor

Books by Vivek Bammi

Golden Buddhism

Indonesia: A Feast for the Senses

Angkor: Celestial Grandeur

Deep Learning: A Journey in Critical Thinking and Reflective Knowledge (co-authored)

JQ: Joy Quotient–Life and Learning after Covid

Journeys to NIRVANA

TRAVEL OPENS THE PATH TO LIBERATION

VIVEK BAMMI

ALEPH BOOK COMPANY
An independent publishing firm
promoted by ***Rupa Publications India***

First published in India in 2025
by Aleph Book Company
161-B/4, Gulmohar House,
Yusuf Sarai Community Centre,
New Delhi 110049

ISBN: 978-93-6523-952-2

1 3 5 7 9 10 8 6 4 2

Printed in India.

Dedicated with love and affection to:

My parents, for a glorious childhood and the gifts of passionate curiosity and joy
Mini, Vihan, and Veer, for our journeys together and the gifts of friendship and love
Bobo and Frank, for opening up so many vistas of life and many laughs
Anjali, for warm friendship and laughter
Manjula and Stuart, Amita and Ted, Bernie Ulozas, my friends for ever
Southie, Nikhil, Harsh, my buddies for life
Shagufta and our travel groups in Uzbekistan and Varanasi, for our amazing adventures, fun times, and celebrations together
Deniek Sukarya and Arun Taneja, my inspiring photography teachers and friends
Jen Olmsted and Frank Thomas, my laughing partners
Dosco class of 1971, forever family
Bammi and Maini clans, for the warmth and beauty of extended family
My students, for the beautiful exchange of thoughts and souls, forever in my heart

'There is no happiness for him who does not travel, Rohita! Living in the society of men, the best man (often) becomes a sinner.... Therefore, wander!... The feet of the wanderer are like the flower, his soul is growing and reaping the fruit.... Therefore, wander!... The fortune of him who is sitting, sits; it rises when he rises; it sleeps when he sleeps; it moves when he moves. Therefore, wander!'

–Lord Indra

'But do not ask me where I am going,
As I travel in this limitless world,
Where every step I take is my home.'

–Dogen Zenji (translated by Steven Heine)

'To be fully alive, fully human, and completely awake is to be continually thrown out of the nest.'

–Pema Chödrön

Contents

Norway fjord: sounds of silence.

Introduction

Wanderlust, the urge to move and travel, belongs in our veins, the core of our inner being. The nerve that runs through our anatomy, the 'vagus', derives its name from the Latin 'to wander'. Wandering is thus part of our biological heredity and instinct. It also derives from our historical heritage, our nomadic ancestors setting us on a path of constant roaming. Divine sanction adds to its aura and appeal. The Indian Vedic god, Lord Indra, is the protector of travellers. He urges his devotees to wander, since 'there is no happiness for him who does not travel'. In our own times, travel has become synonymous with a release from tedious routine, supported by a flourishing leisure industry. Temporarily felled by war or pandemic, the yearning to move reasserts itself as a cathartic release from confinement, reclaiming the human desire for adventure, the joys of exploration and expansion of the circle of life.

Travel has been my loyal and delightful companion since the earliest days. Growing up in the tropical wonderland of Assam in Northeast India triggered an initial encounter with jungle, wildlife, and mighty rivers as much as the manicured tea estates managed by my father and the carefully tended flower and vegetable gardens of my mother. The aesthetic explosion of a glorious childhood found its exhilarating extension in my career as an international student and educator. Interactions with young adults and colleagues from diverse corners of the globe helped dissolve the boundaries that often divide humans, in the animated cauldron of the classroom, the playing field, the theatre, the laboratories of learning. They also paved the way for a thrilling opportunity to discover the richness of natural and human existence in myriad continents.

As the travel bug ensnared me for life, the physical act of movement gradually transformed into a journey of the mind and the soul. I realized the wisdom of Lord Indra's insight that 'the feet of the wanderer are like the flower, his soul is growing and reaping the fruit'. Allied to my sprouting passion for photography, a simultaneous reaping of flower and fruit emanated in a pleasing yin-yang[1]–an active engagement with people and places merging with an enlarged inner space.

This book invites you to share in my enthralling journeys toward nirvana, a feeling of fulfilment and joy with multiple dimensions. In his personal quest, the Buddha liberated himself and countless others from the sorrowful tones of suffering, confidently proclaiming: 'Nirvana is *aroga,* freedom from illness; *shiva*, happiness; *kshema*, security; *abhaya*, the absence of fear; *shanta*, peace of mind; *anashrava*, freedom from compulsions; *ajara*, untouched by age; *amata*, unaffected by death.'[2]

In travel, I discovered another aspect of nirvana: liberation from the confinement of social and cultural conditioning—everything that traps us within narrow walls of experience, thought, and worldview. My explorations resulted in expansive delight, replete with striking images, serendipity, and the warmth of human interaction in diverse corners of the globe.

Combining pictures and written passages, this book can be treated as a series of meditative insights, or as a symphony with recurring motifs with variation as well as an organic unity. The reader is also directed to accessible musical passages that enhance the sensory experience of place.

From my earliest explorations, nature remains the greatest inspiration, its aesthetic grandeur matched by profound lessons in harmony and humility. Its creative juices find resonance in our artistic impulse, mirroring a display of diversity and flourishing. The human imagination has soared in celebration of this infinite bounty, each expression lighting up a facet of existence, enriching our emotions and the search for a meaningful connection with others. Whether in drawing, song, food, decoration, or love—humans thrive in exchange, setting up civilizations of exquisite structures and taste. Periods of separation and aloneness also germinate intense awareness and understanding. Finding attunement with impermanence and changing vistas, we discover the freedom to carve a pace and path in consonance with our own pulse.

A traveller navigates every sensation, enters deeply into each episode, reaching toward a state of full awakening. To be awake is to experience a passionate existence in a constant state of curiosity and wonder.

This is a richness beyond compare, the fulfilment of life itself.

Norway fjord: alchemy of elements.

Norway fjord: whispers of Creation.

Nature: a Journey in Awe and Humility

'The Dao is the way of balance and harmony.'
—Lao Tzu[1]

Ever since a school Geography lesson, the fjords of Norway—unique and spectacular contours of Creation—had beckoned me. Nothing, though, could prepare us for the spectacle unfolding before our eyes as we traversed the Sognefjord and Hardangerfjord. The symphony of water, land, mountain, forest, and sky makes for unrivalled splendour. Human habitations appear as mere specks amidst this awesome majesty,

Norway fjord: symphony of water, land, and sky.

a reminder of our insignificance in the cosmic drama. Chinese landscape paintings from the earliest stages of their civilization captured the minute scale of human structures and existence in contrast to the might of nature.

Yet, ancient Chinese and modern Norwegians learnt to live in harmony with the grand forces, born from a reverence for this gift from a higher power.

What struck me most at the fjords was an overwhelming sense of silence, an enormous stillness amidst the movement of clouds and water. It seemed that we were witnessing the moments before Creation, or perhaps its first whispers.

Norway fjord: harmony of nature and humans.

In the tradition of Chinese landscape painting, the forces of nature tower over human elements like buildings and bridges, reinforcing our insignificance in the cosmic scale, but also the ability to live in harmony with the elements. Photo by Peter Griffin.

Alpine landscape, Switzerland.

Alpine scenery, Switzerland.

Meadow, Switzerland.

Train journeys across Alpine Switzerland, Austria, and Slovenia reveal changing vistas, competing for visual and visceral delight. Snowy patches on mountain-tops occasionally descend and plunge into azure waters, while brooks and streams flow along in energetic ripples. Lush meadows, often clothed in flushing flowery patterns and graced with the presence of contented bovines, complete the picture of a sylvan idyll. Lakes, reflecting the pride and grace of their hilly companions, invite us to break into celebratory song.

The pace of rail travel is the perfect counterpoint to the frenzied rhythms of modern living. There is space for contemplation and imagination; even storytelling on the ever-transforming relationship of clouds and peaks, of lakes and rivers, of animals and humans. An unhurried 'andante'[2] creates a melody of serene repose.

Meadow, Switzerland: bovine contentment.

Halstatt village, Austria.

Lake Bled and Castle, Slovenia.

Sonamarg glacier, Kashmir, India.

An even more leisurely tempo, on horseback, brings one to the thrall of mountain-scapes amidst the pristine beauty of Kashmir.[3] Glaciers proclaim their frosty glory, sentinels for their summits as much as the reservoir of precious liquid for thirsty humans and lands in their shadow. When the fluid turns milky, frolicking with the rocks at Doodhpathri, we marvel at the aesthetic instinct that finds resonance in human souls. Observing the unparalleled artistry of nature in Kashmir, Mughal emperors and poets recognized it as a slice of paradise offered for our rapture on Earth.

Shepherd's hut in Gulmarg, Kashmir, India.

Doodhpathri (Valley of Milk), Kashmir, India.

Away from movement and in the calm of rapt attention, we gaze in awe at another spectacle of unfolding majesty, embracing us in its noble presence. An early-morning view of the Kanchendzonga and sister Himalayan ranges promises the dawn of an expansive consciousness, linking our tiny pulsations to a transcendent architect, shaping the foundations of our existence and demanding our obeisance in return.

Any illusion we may have about the solidity and permanence of mountains, though, is quickly dispelled at the Zhangye Danxia Landform Park in China's Gansu province. The aptly named Rainbow Mountains offer a startling palette of hues crafted over millions of years of chemical ferment. The magical alchemy on display here would defeat any human artist's attempt at capturing it. As if to underline this point, the crusty stones at the site have constructed a castle nearly 20 metres higher than the Louvre, the repository of some of humanity's greatest artworks.

I am reminded here of the remarkable insights from Japanese Zen, which alter our perspectives based on profound observations of natural forces: those that appear stable and changeless are in fact in a state of perpetual churn, nurturing the lifeline to other forms which partake freely of the comfort of this bounty. The aesthetic flair of the elements adds to our veneration.

Kanchendzonga and sister ranges: view from Pelling, Sikkim, India

Rainbow Mountains, Zhangye Danxia, China.

The Louvre castle, Zhangye Danxia, China.

Huangshan (Yellow Mountains), China.

Mountains continue as sources of inspiration and guidance in several cultures. The Huangshan (Yellow Mountains) in China abounds in lofty pinnacles which have animated the brushes of artists through the centuries, preserving the eternal message of Lao Tzu that the Dao, or the path to learning, flows from an intimate grasp of nature's rhythms, which are unhurried yet achieve a balance and harmony of its elements. Art, too, moves toward coherence and fulfilment in all forms through patient effort.

For the Japanese, nature is imbued with the vitality of the 'kami' spirits that have protected and nourished their exquisite land from the beginning of time, framing the practices of Shinto, their original faith. The most exalted status belongs to Mount Fuji, a boon for worshippers and artists alike in its perfect symmetry. Having marvelled at the images of Hiroshige and Hokusai,[4] my sighting of Fuji San felt like the consummation of a spiritual tryst. As Zen had intuited, this summit moved in the veins of my inner landscape.

View of Mount Fuji from Hakone, Japan. The Torii gate indicates the entry to a Shinto shrine, marking the Japanese reverence for nature.

While we gasp at the lofty magnificence and grace of montane landscapes, we are equally dazzled by the immensity and depth of oceanic vistas. At the Hokkaido island, I was treated to an azure masterpiece from the Sea of Japan, pointing to the vast expanse of the Pacific, our grandest marine entity. Sky and water combine to create the gleaming 'Shokutan blue' (named after the area), but nature orchestrates more of its artistic genius in the rock formations, arising in angular glory from the seabed. As with any artist, we delight in endless variation in shape and line.

'Shokutan blue' at the Sea of Japan, Hokkaido island.

We are reminded that, far from its seeming fragility, water, in fact, carries the power to overwhelm and sculpt other elements to its palate. The *Dao de Jing*, a seminal text of Chinese civilization, avers: 'Nothing in the world is as soft and weak as water and yet in attacking what is hard and strong, nothing can surpass it.'[5]

The sea has overwhelmed human monuments, even entire cities, with its eternal tenacity. This capability is narrated in a Breton myth of a cathedral that was submerged off the island of Ys, which inspired a stunning piano composition, 'The Engulfed Cathedral' by the French composer Claude Debussy.[6]

Through the morphing tones and moods of the work we can envisage the reappearance of the cathedral, with its bells and the resounding organ, before it is engulfed again by the mighty power of water.

Recalling Lao Tzu, water adheres to its own pace of patient effort.

Sea of Japan, Hokkaido island.

Cathedral 1, Postojna Caves, Slovenia.

Over centuries, this can result in scenes of staggering splendour, as I discovered at the Postojna caves in Slovenia. The stalagmites and stalactites here have conjured a complementary dance, built upon the movements of individual liquid drops in choreography reminiscent of renowned ballet dancers Nijinsky and Nureyev. Natural cathedrals thus emerge in carved wonder, to survive the test of time.

The audacity and elegance of water reappears at exquisite spots

Cathedral 2, Postojna Caves, Slovenia.

Filigree pillar, Postojna Caves, Slovenia.

around the globe. The Vøringsfossen waterfall near Geilo, Norway, displays a gushing partnership of liquid and solid, the cascades watched in admiration by rock and humans alike.

Vøringsfossen Waterfall, Norway.

Magical moment: Vøringsfossen Waterfall, Norway.

Abstract artist: Vøringsfossen Waterfall, Norway.

To add to the majesty of the scene, the sun decided to make its presence felt and we were treated to an astonishing rainbow. The vibrant colours and shapes conjured up the outlines of abstract art, every photographer's dream.

The humming water resonates with our inner channels, creating a melody of calm repose.

Meditating at Kuang Si Waterfall, near Luang Prabang, Laos.

Rock garden: Zen temple, Kamakura, Japan.

With their inimitable sense of preserving yet enhancing the course of nature, the Japanese introduce elements of flow and perspective at the Zen garden. Here, water is represented by patterns of granular wavy sand in companionship with rocks of varying size. The sand is raked regularly, creating the illusion of motion and flux. In zazen (sitting meditation), we are invited to observe the play of permanence (stone) and impermanence (sand), of stillness and movement, contrasting yet coalescing elements of life's pulse.

Forests have attracted humans since aeons, emanating mystical power and abundance. In our hurried and anxious times, they hold the promise of a healing touch, a protective aura. The Japanese advise shinrin-yoku, or forest-bathing, to cleanse the impurities of emotion and soul. When mist drifts into the woods, we achieve a primeval release from everyday reality, merging with the energy of the nurturing spirit.

Artists in Asian cultures are particularly inspired by the tensile flexibility of bamboo, shaping its malleable timber while revering its resilience and fortitude.

Forest-bathing: Kurseong, West Bengal, India.

Bamboo forest temple: Kamakura, Japan.

Forest of faith, Sagrada Família, Barcelona, Spain.

Spanish architect Antoni Gaudi brought the forest into his grand conception of the Sagrada Família in Barcelona. The interior columns in this magnificent cathedral taper heavenward, reminiscent of trees as they ascend toward sacred space. Gaudi created a synthesis of his deep Catholic faith and the earliest human intuition to worship the guardians of the bountiful Earth.

Recent scientific studies of forests and trees provide fascinating insights on their ability to collaborate with each other and to live in harmony with the cycle of life. Suzanne Simard, observing paper birch and Douglas fir forests in British Columbia (Canada), found that 'hub' or 'mother' trees nurture their young by sending excess carbon to seedlings through a network, increasing their rate of survival. Mother trees also seem to recognize their 'kin', sending more carbon to their species and reducing root competition to make elbow room for their growth. When dying, they convey their wisdom to the next generation with defence signals that would increase their resilience and resistance to future stresses.[7]

Forests are our teachers as much as healers, underlining the urgent need to protect them from mindless felling to satisfy human greed.

Perhaps no other artist expressed gratitude in the power of healing with the same intensity and magnitude as my favourite composer, Ludwig van Beethoven.[8] In the third movement of his String Quartet No. 15, Beethoven used the Lydian mode, associated with healing and recovery, to create sounds that pierce the soul with tenderness and cheerful thanksgiving. Not surprisingly, he was a great lover of nature and its capacity to rejuvenate the human spirit.

Probably the most intimidating form of creation with their vast expanses of seeming emptiness, deserts exert a fascination for the explorer, adventurer, and tourist alike. With courage and determination, humans have overcome the travails of arid immensity in the company of the faithful camel, to exchange goods, beliefs, and stories.

As if to compensate for the dreary terrain, nature imbues the sand with a golden sheen and humans exhibit a colourful burst with their costumes and instruments in an aesthetic counterpoint.

At the Thar in Rajasthan, India, polychrome turbans and glittering jewels mingle with the sounds of the most precious resource in the desert—the first drops of rain, bringing renewal to parched life and spirit.[9]

Gobi Desert, Dunhuang, China.

Not just humans, all life forms need just a smidgen of moisture to release their creative spirit. Desert blooms add to the riotous symphony of sun, sand, and ocean in California, US, turning it into the land of universal fantasy.

Thar Desert, Rajasthan, India.

Desert choreography, San Diego, California, US.

Desert splash, Santa Barbara Mission, California, US.

Often foreboding and grand, nature also offers us the most intimate and fragrant companionship and we celebrate it with careful cultivation and tending. At the exquisite gardens near Bolzano and Trento in northern Italy, riotous colours frame the montane backdrop in aesthetic perfection.

At a more cosy level, we may strike up an affectionate chord with flowers, recalling the poetic reveries of haiku master Matsuo Basho (1644–1694) on the violet and the nazunia.

On the violet:
Violets
By the mountain path:
There's something humble about them.[10]

On the nazunia:
When I look carefully
I see the nazunia blooming
by the hedge![11]

The humility of the violet, displaying its dazzling brilliance for the benefit of all creatures, sprouts empathy in the poet, who discovers his modesty too in observing the 'ordinary' nazunia. It grows effortlessly by the wayside, easy to overlook when compared to the beauty of other blooms. By turning his rapt attention to this unassuming plant, Basho achieves utter absorption. As the Indian mystic Osho sees it: 'If a nazunia can contain such poetry, then each stone can become a sermon…. Rather than possessing the flower, he is possessed by the flower.'[12]

In the beauty of the moment, there is no distance from the elemental forces that have shaped us from the beginning of existence. Our intuition confirms oneness and connectedness, a completion of nature's pulse within.

Giardino di Pojega, near Trento, northern Italy.

Violets: Giardino di Pojega, near Trento, northern Italy.

Humble mountain flower: Balestrand, Norway.

The Arts: a Journey in Wonder and Catharsis

'We are all a deeply aesthetic people.'

—Thupten Jinpa[1]

From the first splashes on rocky outcrops and cave walls, the melodies inspired by birdsong and community spirit, humans have craved an expression of inner spirit and breath. Perhaps, the nomadic trekking and wandering of our ancestors, coupled with the awareness of the brevity of existence, animated the desire to leave an enduring signature for all who followed. They transmitted a veritable feast for the gratified traveller today.

We can behold astonishing clarity of line, colour, and conception in the rocks and caves of aboriginal Australia, Indonesia, India, and Africa, the sanctuaries of Lascaux and Altamira in Europe. They bear witness to a universal explosion of the human mind as far back as 40,000 to 50,000 years ago. We may speculate on the motivating force—a magical transference of power to ensure success in the search for food, a ritual of worship or adoration of animals and natural forces, a trance-like splurge of imagination, or perhaps the origins of leisure-time entertainment. Ultimately, though, these are spectacles of current delight.

With their keen awareness of the vitality of energy flowing in all surrounding forms, early humans equated the stability of rock with the quest for permanence amidst the reality of fragility. The dolmens seem to be an initial attempt to prolong remembrance of the spark of life, add new dimensions in the quest for continuity, and appeal to celestial grace. We may see here the foundations of the grandeur that later emerged in the pyramids and in Stonehenge, temples to faith and extensions of time. A lingering mystical element preserves our sense of wonder at our earliest builders.

Hunting scene: Anegundi rock painting, near Hampi, Karnataka, India. Made with natural pigments, this is an extraordinarily dynamic example of primitive art—animals and humans portrayed in suspended motion. The circular motifs at the top-centre could be a magical talisman or an early experiment in abstract art by our first artists. The similarities to primitive paintings in other parts of the world are remarkable.

Hooded cobra: Anegundi rock painting, near Hampi, Karnataka, India.

We have always evinced fascination with snakes, and the awesome hooded cobra found its way from animistic beliefs into worship and iconic status in later religions. The human figures at the bottom-left seem to stand transfixed at the imposing sight unfolding in their gaze. Apart from the power of the venom, snakes have captivated us with their ability to slough off old skin and regain a youthful appearance, a source of considerable envy for mortal humans.

Dolmen: near Pattadakal, Karnataka, India.

For nomadic and cave-dwelling early humans, the idea of a permanent shelter would have seemed a distant fantasy. The first attempts at simple walls-and-roof structures may have been dedicated to the forces that enabled survival against the odds of nature and animals. Although the function of the dolmen remains unclear, it is tempting to ascribe to them the status of our earliest sacred space, the home for a power that transcends earthly limits.

Nose flute: Paiwan indigenous group, Taiwan
(at Shung Ye Museum of Formosan Aborigines, Taipei, Taiwan).
'Music became the measure of our breath.'

As with painting and building, we marvel at the eternal partnership of sound and the human soul. The ability of our ancestors to shape bone, wood, metal, and the biological gift of voice into uplifting and consoling song found a resonance in the deepest recesses of our being. This bond has never wavered or diminished, as music became the measure of our breath, the intimate rhythm of existence.

'Male Harp Player of the Early Spedos Type' from the Getty Museum Collection: Cycladic (early Greek) art. A beautiful depiction of the human voice and instrument in harmony.

While animals and nature continued to fascinate and stimulate artists throughout the ages, brush and paint found a particular intrigue in mirroring that most captivating subject of all—the human face. That confined arena seems to reveal the entire range and drama of experience and emotion, even a fleeting glimpse enough to unlock a previously concealed interior. At the hands of a genius like Van Gogh, we enter into the very marrow of time and character, visible at the eponymous museum in the charming lanes of Amsterdam. In his self-portraits, we witness the complete removal of boundaries between the artist and his calling. Every stroke carries this man's intense suffering and his ability to transcend agony with the vitality of an inner fire. Despite his short, tortured existence on Earth, Van Gogh's oeuvre contains the immortal spark stirring our deepest sentiments.[2]

Perhaps no other artist captured existential distress and anxiety with the same acuity as the Norwegian Edvard Munch in his repeated depictions of *The Scream*. Whether in wood-cut or blood-curdling colour waves, we hear the primal wail of anguish echoing through the cosmos.[3]

Yet, through the magic of art, we may begin to see this as a cleansing moment; Munch's universal shriek enables us to bellow out our sorrows and sufferings, to be replaced by kindly creation with sounds of release and equanimity.

Even at their saddest, painting and music carry the power of revival and redemption, stirring the core of our being with the promise of healing. For Van Gogh, as for Beethoven, nature was the refuge, the eternal hope of spring overcoming the shadows of the wintry soul.

For Monet and the Impressionists, nature became the canvas for capturing its ephemeral moods, the dance of light and colour with the changing seasons. In his carefully cultivated garden at Giverny, Monet found the inspiration for bringing us even closer to the act of Creation itself, the brush strokes infused with the primal energy of existence, a world coming into being with the volition of the artist. Achieving confident mastery, he dispensed with almost all artistic conventions to sweep us along into the infinite animation of the elements.[4]

A visit to Giverny is a pilgrimage to the source of creativity, as much as Beethoven's house in Heiligenstadt near Vienna. At both spots, I felt the fulfilment of an aesthetic quest; just as Monet gives us intimations of the spark of luminosity, line, and hue, Beethoven conjures up the magical

Monet's garden at Giverny, France, with the Japanese-style bridge—the scene and inspiration for several of his *Water Lilies* painting series.

mingling of note, tone, and rhythm, with our inner cadence. Both are worthy inheritors of our first artists, comforting and elevating our spirits to realms beyond earthly comprehension. In continuing the partnership between the cosmic and the human, they transcend every limitation imposed by our fragile presence.

At Heiligenstadt, Beethoven contemplated ending his life at the onset of a devastating deafness, but the cauldron of creativity kept his inner flare alive for another twenty-five years, much to the delight and gratitude of generations to follow. In outpourings like his 'Eroica' ('Heroic') symphony, the artist emerges as the true hero, overcoming the most daunting obstacles on the path to liberating expression.[5]

This is not an egotistical journey, though, for Beethoven evokes the vision of the artist bringing all humans together in an enduring fellowship, bound by the uplifting strains of the 'Ode to Joy',[6] overseen by a compassionate Creator.

Just as Monet had blessed us with the infinity of Creation, Beethoven gifted us the infinity of human emotion. As Japanese author Haruki Murakami exults, this is 'music that made you feel like something in the very structure of your body has been reconfigured'.[7]

Ecstatic flow: dancer with anklet, Khajuraho, India.

Another primal instinct, movement, has accompanied sound and rhythm from the earliest traces of the human journey. Probably originating in awe and imitation of the graceful and athletic moves of animals and birds that added colour and food to our survival, dance evolved into a joyous celebration of existence itself. Artists delighted in capturing and creating the flow and energy of the body as it transformed into a dynamic theatre of expression, conveying some of our deepest longing, desire, and understanding.

From the throb of the African jungle to the rap of urban pavement, we are enthralled by beat and gliding motion, echoing the heart's yearning for a release from constraint. In the temple walls of Khajuraho and Badami, as well as the grandeur of the Mughal court,[8] Indian civilization revels in a fusion of dance and music as the celebration of a liberated spirit.

Travel, too, is a dance of elation, our nomadic impulse converted into catharsis.

Having ensured initial survival against daunting odds, humans forged the desire to improve upon our surroundings, to layer a patina of grace, beauty, and elegance upon mundane reality. The craving for design added a pleasing flourish to public and private space, transforming urban-scape and interior expanse alike.

Nyhavn, Copenhagen, Denmark.

Church of Our Saviour, Copenhagen (Christiania), Denmark.

Copenhagen ranks amongst the design and style capitals in my estimation. The pleasing facades at Nyhavn seem to preserve the spirit of Viking adventure and exploration, neatly balanced by the comfort of 'hygge'(a Danish word implying well-being and comfort) on returning home, promising a blend of warmth and bonding (complete with the pet dog or cat) around the family hearth. Similarly, soaring cathedral spires combine with the earthly pleasures of leisurely rides along bicycle-friendly paths.

Uzbek design: the muqarnas or honeycomb eaves are a common feature in Islamic architecture, but their splendour in the mosques and madrassas of Uzbekistan is seldom matched.

Prohibited from the portrayal of humans and animals by scripture, the artisans of Bukhara, Samarkand, and Ferghana in Uzbekistan turned stone, earth, and clay into marvels of pattern and form, an explosion of motifs and colours that dazzle the enchanted eye. In contrast to Milton's *Paradise Lost*, this is 'Paradise Found', carved by the human hand.

Uzbek design: a dazzling interior in the mausoleum of Amir Timur, the historical hero and unifier of the Uzbeks, in Samarkand, Uzbekistan.

The magnificent design of the dome and arch from Amir Timur's mausoleum in Samarkand, Uzbekistan.

Uzbek design: Bibi-Khanum's mosque, Samarkand, Uzbekistan.

Earthy metaphors abound in some of our contemporary design masterpieces. French architect Paul Andreu seems to have found inspiration in one of nature's abiding miracles, the emergence of life from the nurturing womb of the egg. His creation, the National Centre for the Performing Arts in Beijing, is fondly called the Giant Egg, capturing the magical visage of the hemispherical structure and dome resting upon a pool of soothing water. On entering, the illusion of a floating wonder is preserved, the flowing liquid on the roof seeming to defy gravity. The aura of fertility finds its fruition in the concert halls and theatres that reverberate with the sounds and sights of performers from all corners of the world. The embryo of the human mind enlarges here in a pleasurable feast of the senses within a comfortable womb. This 'egg' defies the necessity to hatch, since it contains boundless riches within its lustrous shell, removing all cultural boundaries in a celebration of humanity enveloped in the sounds of passion and harmony.

At the monumental Cloud Gate installation in Chicago, other boundaries begin to dissolve. Here, the Earth's minerals and metals come together to reduce the distance between nature and human construction, but they pose a challenge to some of our most revered notions. As we view our reflections on the curving surface, we are mirrored in an array of changing and convoluting shapes.

National Centre for the Performing Arts, Beijing, China.[9]

Anish Kapoor: Cloud Gate (The Bean) installation, Chicago, US.

Neither the ego nor identity has any sense of permanence or fixed essence here. Sculptor Anish Kapoor has liberated us from the constraining obsession with definition. This generous sphere invites us to chisel our own path, unfettered by custom or compulsion.

Reflections in the Cloud Gate, Chicago, US.

Endless affection: Taj Mahal, Agra, India.

Another art form that demands a diminution of the ego originates in the comforting cocoon of the womb. That ethereal bonding of mother and child finds its endearing extension in the quest for companionship and completion in the 'other'. Love is the aesthetic impulse to discover beauty—of body, mind, soul—and celebrate its fruition in a dazzling variety of expression and emotion. When an emperor loses his soulmate, he decides to immortalize her presence with a masterpiece that resonates in the romantic recesses of every tender bosom. The grandeur of conception of the Taj Mahal finds its complement in the exquisite detail of decoration in stone, gem, water, and plant, refined to utter simplicity in the gravestones of the lovers. In the moonlight, it is suffused with the symphony of endless affection.

When the ingredients come together in a pleasing synthesis, an entire city can radiate a romantic élan. The flair and elegance of buildings matched by the finesse and poise of its citizens, artistic wonders mirrored in the fluid grace of its river, Paris carries the breathless anticipation and consummation of a love affair. The strains of Chopin and Mozart wafting from a pianist's fingers at the Notre-Dame,

The treasure of the City of Light and Love:
Notre-Dame Cathedral, Paris, France.[10]

accompanied by the golden gleam of sunset upon its roseate walls; nearby, boats floating down the Seine in languid sway: this is the pinnacle of 'l'amour', and we are transported into the dreamy embrace of Offenbach's sumptuous song 'Belle nuit ô nuit d'amour' ('Beautiful night—the night of love').[11]

Nuit d'amour: sunset on the river Seine, Paris, France.

Coddled by water to a greater extent than Paris, Venice suggests a jaded yet perennial romance. The canals and stones appear in a state of worn fatigue, the aging complexion accompanied by a sinking anxiety. Yet, the plucky arias of gondoliers and the delighted footfall of entranced visitors ensure a defiant resurgence of youthful vigour, confirming the instincts of traders through the centuries in crowning it the pearl of exchange and connection.

The Doges celebrated with sumptuous palaces, while the Casanova discovered multiple avenues for temporary but artful dalliances.

Venice is opera on a grand scale, and nothing can silence its resilient serenade.

Afternoon chat, Venice, Italy.

The gondolier's aria, Venice, Italy.

Often celebrated as a rapport of individuals, love thrives in the soothing cradle of community too. Bonds of family, village, faith, and practice instilled in childhood flower into warm and confident partnerships spanning multiple generations.

In Theravada Buddhist lands, an early-morning ritual unites believers with novices and monks: the common people placing daily sustenance into the extended bowls. This act of daily generosity builds merit and empathy in the provider, and monks reciprocate with compassionate counsel and wisdom.

Witnessing this practice, called the Tak Bat, at dawn in Luang Prabang attested to the vibrations of genial caring that emanate from this uplifting spot.

Tak Bat (also called Sai Bat), Luang Prabang, Laos.

Children in Bali have a privileged start in life. For the first six months, they are entwined with the parent and kept away from contact with the ground, as they are believed to have come bearing the imprint of heaven and an angelic tread. The ties with community continue as lifelong links, nourishing a uniquely amiable and assured personality that complements the alluring tropical terrain. The child discovers early inclusion in the exuberant arts of the island, the aesthetic impulse imprinted in the veins.

The shared responsibility of gotong-royong or mutual collaboration finds expression in diverse arenas in Bali. Male orchestras fill the air with the fervent chants of the Kecak chorus, accompanying the dramatic episodes of the Ramayana. Skilful irrigation systems, perfected over centuries, ensure bountiful harvests for the community and the beam in the elderly farmer's eyes as he clutches the stalks of abundance.

Young performer, Bali, Indonesia.

The sheer delight and exuberance of this improvised artistic moment sums up the allure of the island and its people.

Maternal embrace, Bali, Indonesia.

Ceremonial offering, Bali, Indonesia: women play a vital role in preparing and carrying offerings for religious or community events.

Kecak chant: Uluwatu temple, Bali, Indonesia.

The male chorus accompanies the choreographed story of the Ramayana with rhythmic and hypnotic chanting, adding to the dramatic setting of a cliff-side temple at sunset.

Abundance: Bali (Indonesia) farmer.

Love is indeed a many-splendoured thing, as Han Suyin reminded us.[12] At the stunning sculptural panels of the Khajuraho temples in central India, built in the ninth and tenth centuries CE, we witness an uninhibited celebration of human vitality in a state of utter plenitude and pleasure. Sex and eroticism, far from being negated or regarded with moral disdain, are portrayed as joyful instincts and sources of unbounded delight. The Hindu builders honour the feminine power or shakti as the energizing source of Creation. The walls at Khajuraho are replete with the beauty and vigour of women, whether as the Goddess or the intimate human companion. They also echo the Hindu conception of the human drama as a microcosm of the macrocosmic theatre, all forms of life participating in lila, or the playful sport of the gods, introducing 'elements of spontaneity and freedom into the universe'.[13] The variety of erotic practices depicted enter into this unconstrained licence, but without a trace of vulgarity, for the faces are bathed in a serene joy.

Pleasure abounds, too, in satisfying another primal appetite birthed in the womb. From its origin as nourishment, food has enmeshed itself into history, culture, and every conceivable emotion. It is the rasa or essence of life itself, but when elevated to the art of cuisine, it becomes the embodiment of taste and refined sophistication.

Lucknow, in the plains of northern India, became the coalescing palette of two grand civilizations, melding the genteel Persian passion with the spicy onslaught of Indian herb, fruit, and vegetation. The mutton of the gelawati kabab underwent the softening impact of the papaya rind, resulting in a melting masterpiece. Folklore attributes this mouth-melody to the elegant stricture of a Persian prince, seeking to avoid unseemly chewing sounds in august company. The silence of etiquette was balanced by the flowing conversation among guests seated along the dastarkhwan (banquet spread). The dining ritual in Awadh became the gateway to urbane hospitality and polite community. Couplets in Persian and Urdu inscribed on the dastarkhwan added poetic and philosophical overtones to the experience.

Lucknow manages to preserve its tehzeeb and adab[14] in homes and street kitchens today, along with a repertoire of delicacies contributing to a sensual feast. Murad Ali, undaunted by the loss of an arm, crafted the tundai (literally meaning one-limbed) kabab upon coal embers, a slightly weightier version of the gelawati. The bawarchi khane (home kitchens)

Bacchanalia: stone sculpture, Khajuraho, India.

compete to create exquisite versions of qorma and nehari (richly curried meat dishes), exuding the bewitching aroma of opulent seasoning.

Kabab and curry must blend with a bewildering choice of grainy companions. The tandoori roti swells with the baked assurance of the clay oven, but the naan, the rumali, and the sheermal offer contending options of size, consistency, and sweetening. At the pulao wali gali (named after a lane with expert rice cooks), families continue the tradition of early-morning steaming of Basmati grain, the ethereal fragrance of its kernels combining with earthy ingredients in the captivating symphony of the biryani.

The melt-in-your-mouth gelawati kabab with garnish, Lucknow, India.

The decadent sheen of nehari, from the kitchen of Mubeen's, a renowned hole-in-the wall eatery in the lanes of Lucknow's (India) inner city.

Not that the sweet tooth should be neglected: the Basmati reappears in the swirl of milk, cardamom, and saffron, creating the golden rapture of the phirni. The halwa, too, moulds its elements—egg, flour, or the purple carrot (a winter speciality)—to the demands of its lavish texture. The requirement of a digestive after the calorie overload leads to the introduction of the paan with its carefully crafted contours. The betel leaf has become the symbol of exchange in many Asian cultures, an accompaniment in marriage rites as much as an essential feature in customary repasts. Paan completes the circle of cordial dining in Lucknow with a flourish.

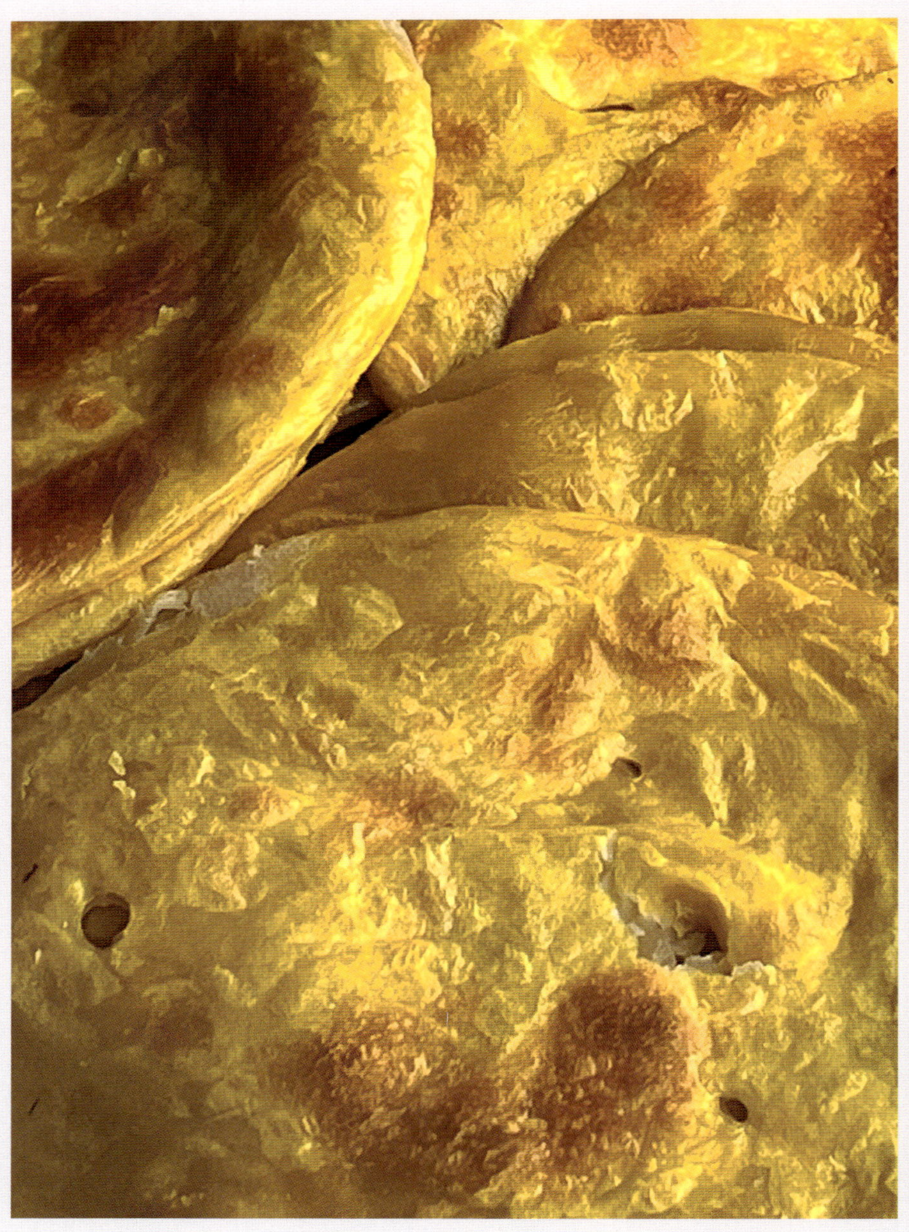

The golden crust of sheermal roti,
with just a hint of sweetening, Lucknow, India.

The luscious, saffron-induced thrill of phirni, Lucknow, India.

The ingredients transformed into the addictive paan, Lucknow, India.

In the Mediterranean lands, a similar gustatory ambience adds lustre to the sunny disposition and healthy intake of the locals. The leisurely pace attunes to laughter, liquor, and light-hearted banter at the dinner table, whose fare is attested by experts today as the superior brain-friendly diet.[15] The cornucopia of the Earth's riches is relished here, with a daily intake of fruits, vegetables, grains, nuts, and dairy, along with weekly consumption of legumes, lean red meat, poultry, fish, and eggs. A Mediterranean dessert ranges from the fermented restraint of Greek yoghurt to the sinful excess of the Italian tiramisu. The presiding deity Bacchus looks on indulgently at the free-flowing scarlet elixir, replete with the blessing of resveratrol[16] released from the juices of the generous grape.

The creamy extravagance of tiramisu
(literally meaning 'pick me up') at Padua, Italy.

Joyful dining at Piazza Santa Lucia, Venice, Italy.

Scarlet elixir at the streets of Venice, Italy.

The evening passeggiata in Italy brings friends, acquaintances, and strangers together in bonhomie around the delightful vistas of piazzas and their historical footprints.

Food, wine, amiable companionship: the art of love has reached its zenith, for we are now in harmony with the richness and passion of life.

Exchange: a Journey in Endurance and Efflorescence

'In my eyes, a country's enthusiasm for other customs was the mark of a great civilization that could absorb every difference.'

—Chinese empress Wu[1]

From the first audacious and daring steps of our African ancestors, no obstacle deterred *Homo sapiens* from traversing unfamiliar domains and leaving an indelible imprint upon our collective soul. The discovery that interaction with the 'other' would enrich and transform our being became the recurring celebratory motif of humanity at its best.

With our hardy humped companion, we overcame the travails of scorching heat, numbing cold, and parched throats to create a thriving artery of goods and ideas, stretching between the glorious civilizations of China, India, and Rome for over a thousand years. In Shan Sa's book *Empress: A Novel*, Chinese empress Wu Zetian (624–705 CE), the only female ruler in the country's history, marvels at the way in which the outsiders' craving for silk and porcelain transformed the comfort levels and lifestyles of the Chinese themselves: 'High-level chairs and tables and raised beds allowed us to stretch our legs. The music from the oasis conquered us with its powerful impulsive rhythms. The twirling dances from those parts—so different from the Chinese dances that included restricted and graceful slowness and ritual gestures—showed us all the beauty of spontaneity.'[2]

The mind was inevitably stirred by these flowing currents. Universal faiths—Buddhism, Christianity, Islam—found fertile echoes in the desert silences. Deep in the Gobi, the caves at Dunhuang preserve the eternal message of the Great Liberator amidst scenes of artistry (much like the Buddhist cave paintings at Ajanta in western India). The uplifting strains of celestial music augment the soothing reassurance of the Buddha's path to joyful living on Earth.

The Buddha's reassurance: Dunhuang (Mogao) cave painting, China (fifth century CE).

Celestial music: Dunhuang (Mogao) cave painting,
China (Tang dynasty period, 618–907 CE).

The resplendent haveli (mansion) of a Jaisalmer (Rajasthan, India) merchant, where the lustre of the local golden sandstone combines with extravagant carving, built upon the riches of Silk Road trade and exchange.

In another arid setting, the Thar, Jaisalmer dazzles with the golden glow of its quarries. Profiting handsomely off the exchanges along the Silk Highway, traders and nobles turned Jaisalmer into a wonderland of exquisite walls, windows, doors of latticed intricacy, and resplendent décor. The welcoming demeanour of its citizens conserves centuries of hospitality, warm hearts complementing cosy hearths with pleasant desert fare.

Extravagant brackets and eaves, Jaisalmer, India:perfect for desert ventilation, with arches reminiscent of distant Rome.

A jharoka (window), Jaisalmer, India: the consummate viewing platform for street ceremonies and festivals.

A been player, Jaisalmer, India: the shape and sound evoke great similarity to the Scottish bagpipe, with a hint of Tartan in the colourful clothing and cover—perhaps a more recent cultural exchange between India and Europe.

Mystical air: Itchan Kala (walled inner city), Khiva, Uzbekistan. The walls provided protection for traders and their caravans on the arduous Silk Road.

The companionship of oasis and desert enabled the blooming of vibrant nodes of commerce and artistry. Khiva, Bukhara, and Samarkand sparkle with flamboyant masterpieces as much as covert stones and alleyways guarding tales of imperial glory, fervent faith, abiding wisdom, and resilient survival.

A statue depicting friendship and exchange enlivens the crisp night air in Khiva, Uzbekistan.

Sublime brick: Maqbara (mausoleum) of Ismoil Samoniy, Bukhara, Uzbekistan. This unique structure is part of Bukhara's masterpiece haven.

Gilded splendour: the Tilla-Kari madrassa, Registan Square, Samarkand, Uzbekistan.

Bibi-Khanum Mosque, Samarkand, Uzbekistan:
built by the Chinese wife of Amir Timur (1336–1405).

Registan Square, Samarkand, Uzbekistan.

The madrassas and mosques of Uzbek glory resonate with the transcendent rhythms of scripture, exalting both the Almighty and the quest of the human intellect to unearth the deepest layers of thought and understanding. I have seldom felt a greater celebration of the spirit, in all its radiant dimensions, than at these three spots. A mystical ambience combines with splashes of exotic turquoise, mustard, blues, greens, reds, and black, upon stone lovingly shaped to display the genius of the artist and the ruler, albeit pale imitations of the majesty of the Creator.

Samarkand's Registan Square invites the entire world to revel in its aesthetic and spiritual wonderland. It has not just been a crossroads for the mingling of humanity and civilizations through the aeons; for me, Samarkand is also a meeting point for souls, where every strand of history and exchange comes together in a pleasing and emotional synthesis.

Just as land obstacles did not deter the quest for exploration and transaction, oceanic depths too were overcome in the search for novel harvests. The influence of new ideas and beliefs could occasionally create a magnificence overshadowing the original in imagination and execution. At Angkor, Hindu and Buddhist conceptions from India flowered in matchless glory, as Khmer builders vied for grandeur on a scale that left posterity gasping in admiration.

The Battle of Kurukshetra from the Mahabharata: Angkor Wat, Cambodia (built in 1116–1150 CE). Vestiges of original paint remain.

Angkor Thom, the dramatic entry to the Bayon at Angkor (Cambodia) with its smiling Buddha-like images.

Masked performers at the Bayon, Angkor, Cambodia.

Nataraja, or Lord Shiva as the cosmic dancer: Banteay Srei, Angkor, Cambodia.

Angkor Wat recreated the celestial Hindu realm of Mount Meru with heavenly apsara (angel) visages floating down the walls, depicting epic scenes from the Mahabharata. At the Bayon, Khmer rulers melded their temporal power with the serene gaze of internal contentment and liberation inspired by a fellow prince, Siddhartha Gautama the Buddha.

The aesthetic flourish of the cosmic dancer, Lord Shiva,[3] finds its ultimate expression in the pink sandstone of Banteay Srei, among the

Ta Prohm, Angkor, Cambodia: the forest co-exists with human creation.

gems of Angkor invention. Another dance unfolds before us at Ta Prohm, as trees and temples intertwine in a dramatic pas de deux. The forest conveys a reminder of the fragility of human pride and achievement, but for the moment, it permits us the pleasure of coexistence.

Another natural peril almost obliterated the grandest Buddhist masterpiece in the world. Volcanic ash from the surrounding montane cauldrons buried the instructive narrative of Borobudur's[4] stone for

Borobudur Temple, Java, Indonesia: scenes from the Buddha's life and journey to enlightenment.

centuries, but we can thankfully engage with its uplifting journey again. At the base and lower levels, the walls speak of samsara, the reality of beings ensnared in the coils of existential struggle, angst, and suffering. As we move upward, we gain inspiration from sculptures depicting the

The pinnacle: Borobudur Temple, Java, Indonesia.

life and transformation of the Buddha and the Bodhisattvas, emanating an inclusive embrace of compassion for all sentient beings in their quest for freedom from suffering. The ascent to the summit concludes the pilgrimage to liberation in an ambience of equanimity and serenity. Circular stupas, the shape of completion, preserve the treasured teaching for eternity. Ensconced in the stupa, the meditative Buddha creates a magnificent symphonic pinnacle with a neighbouring peak, now a tranquil witness to the ultimate truth.

In a remarkable feat of Indian and Indonesian interaction, echoing the Khmer in Cambodia, Hindu and Buddhist streams mingled freely with indigenous waters. A short distance from the Borobudur, at

Yogyakarta, the Prambanan Temples proclaim the nobility of the Hindu trinity of Brahma, Vishnu, and Shiva. This city in Java is also a contemporary centre of Islamic learning, while continuing to radiate the wisdom of the Kraton palace, the repository of traditional etiquette and lifestyle. The core of Javanese practice emerges from the opposition of 'halus' (meaning refined) and 'kasar' (meaning crude), with the sultan[5] and the aristocracy enjoined as exemplars of halus speech and behaviour. Figures from the Mahabharata play their role as well, the virtuous princess Sembadra setting the tone with 'words and actions as sweet as sugar water'. At the fragrant tlampok tree within the palace, the sultan is reminded of the Javanese perfume of goodness: 'Speak always nicely, so your name will be famous all over the world.'[6]

The aura of mellow civility and respectful interaction permeates Indonesia, making it one of the happiest corners of the globe that I've come across.

I realized that, through the centuries of humans mingling with each other, what matters most is the exchange of courtesy and a smile. I found that most readily in Indonesia.

Separation and Loss: a Journey in Solitude and Resilience

'Being alone
may also be pleasant—
autumn dusk.'

—Yosa Buson[1]

The blossoming of new friendships is among the traveller's most cherished joys. However, one must also confront periods of isolation and solitude in negotiating strange lands, tongues, and customs in unfamiliar settings. Although daunting at times, these moments can turn into fertile avenues of self-discovery and engagement with deeper sources of inspiration.

The Buddhist scholar and teacher Stephen Batchelor celebrates solitude as 'a site of autonomy, wonder, contemplation, imagination, inspiration, and care', an art form in itself. We become comfortable in patience and silence: 'Don't expect anything to happen. Just wait. This waiting is a deep acceptance of the moment as such…unquestioning love of whatever has fated you to be here.'[2]

Silence creates the possibility of an awakening: 'Ask "What is this?" then open yourself completely to what you "hear" in the silence that follows. Be open to this question in the same way as you would listen to a piece of music. Pay total attention to the polyphony of the birds and wind outside, the occasional plane that flies overhead, the patter of rain on a window. Listen carefully, and notice how listening is not just an opening of the mind but an opening of the heart, a vital concern or care for the world.'[3]

Solitude: Balestrand, Norway.

Contemplation: Angkor, Cambodia.

Dramatic escape: Kuldhara, Rajasthan, India.

Faded artistry: Kuldhara, Rajasthan, India.

Silence and contemplation also enable a delving into our inner essence and to confront our reality. Buddhist scholar Lama Alan Wallace reminds us of two types of happiness: the pursuit of wealth, power, and prestige, which generates transient pleasure; and 'eudaimonia', an authentic well-being rooted in the ethics of non-violence and benevolence. For the individual as much for the world, cultivating a sense of balance and sustainable living becomes the restorative we must adopt for the survival of our planet.

A transformed outlook and practice remain within grasp, for intervals of solitude and deep reflection sprout 'the ability to see each moment as a chance to start anew, to savour life as ongoing, unfixed, ever-changing and ever capable of being changed'.[4]

The traveller can resume mobility with an expanded and adaptable mind, open to every experience crossing the path ahead, aware of our collective responsibility towards all of Creation.

Just as periods of isolation and solitude foster renewal, images of loss can stir the imagination and avenues of empathy. At Kuldhara, near Jaisalmer in the Thar desert, we come across abandoned vistas of hearths and faith. The fragmented walls whisper the tale of a village deserted overnight to protect the daughter of the village chief from the then-ruler of Jaisalmer, Salim Singh. No trace of their intended destination or fate remains, yet they left behind stirring footprints of courage, sacrifice, and honour.

Treading through domestic spaces, the laughter and chatter of Kuldhara denizens come alive, as much as the stealth and strategy of the great escape. The skilled hands of artisans and artists continue to cast their colourful contours on the faded facades. Perhaps we were destined to rescue their story from obscurity and extend it to eternity.

Hearth-felt tales: Kuldhara, Rajasthan, India

We may get to recreate music and prayer at another striking relic, the Shettihalli Rosary Church in Karnataka. The skeletal remains of Gothic splendour evoke the sounds of psalms and sermons emanating from the pulpit, the nave, and the pews. The monumental chords of the organ blend with the fragrance of myrrh in our imaginative space.

A nearby dam partly submerges the church in water every monsoon, a reminder of the whimsical tides of history. However, unlike the cathedral at Ys island immortalized in Debussy's notes, the Rosary resurrects itself in the drier months and the beads of devotion resume their murmur amidst the wizened pillars.

Imposing facade: Shettihalli Rosary Church, Karnataka, India.

Arch of devotion, Shettihalli Rosary Church, Karnataka, India.

Contented faith: Shettihalli Rosary Church, Karnataka, India. Cows graze in the shadow of the imposing exterior, adding a note of tranquillity.

Loss turns into a celebratory dance of continuity within impermanence.

Impermanence: a Journey in Fluidity and Transience

'...all eternity
is in the moment....'

—Mary Oliver

Few sights can rival that of a skilled athlete in motion. We marvel at the dexterity and suppleness of the human body, honed to a breathtaking level of grace and power. Sport teaches us to savour the beauty of the moment, since we may never witness a matching spectacle again. Even after the moment is gone, it leaves us suffused with the joy of movement and its echoes in our own urges to stretch and stride. The passage of time carries its own fulfilment.

Nature offers an even more exquisite pageant of the thrill of artistry within transience. Winter may appear as the bleak season with withered woods and dark skies, but German writer Rainer Maria Rilke considers it as the occasion for nurturing one's inner garden. Memories and experiences can be tempered in the calm embers of contemplation, a balm for the soul and a contrast to the frenetic pace of modern living. When the heavens choose to sprinkle the Earth with dainty flakes in ivory hue, a magical wonderland emerges in an uplifting melody, captured in rapture by the Russian composer Tchaikovsky in his beloved ballet, 'The Nutcracker'.[1]

As voices merge with the deft frames gliding across the stage, Tchaikovsky dispels any gloomy notions of winter, transforming it into celestial delight.

Fence-sitter: Tashkent, Uzbekistan.

Sculpture: Tashkent, Uzbekistan.

Perpetual remembrance: war memorial, Tashkent, Uzbekistan.

Winter conceals other treasures. The Chinese celebrate their new year in the depths of the season, aware that buds of new life are being prepared by the nourishing moisture lurking within the frigid soil. The inner garden longs to blossom, too, within the warm embrace of family and community.

As the miraculous rebirth of leaf and flower awakens the dormant spirit, our hearts, too, become expansive. The Japanese revel in cherry blooms in streets and parks. Zen poet Kobayashi Issa (1763–1828) notices,

> Cherry trees:
> Contemplating their beauty,
> Strangers are like friends.[2]

The spring in the step unites all in the spirit of revived companionship and we yearn for a creative spark mirroring the bountiful Earth.

Spring blossom: Bukhara, Uzbekistan.

Spring blossoms:
Ferghana, Uzbekistan.

The summer of learning: Harvard University, Cambridge, US.

Engulfed in sunshine and warmth, the fragile tendrils discover their footing and delight in the juices of summer, the pale pastels replaced by blazing tints of emerald. The mind geminates into fertile branching and abundance.

The symphony of tree and brick on a summer morning at the buildings in Harvard create an ambience of euphoria. Here we can feel the joy of learning emanating from leaf and wall, the quest of the human brain united with the lush setting. Youngsters and adults from all corners

Summer pleasures: Harvard University, Cambridge, US.

of the globe throng the pathways, celebrating the thriving of insight, wit, and wisdom in their midst.

Summer ensures feasting on fruit and grain, after which the air modulates to a bracing chill. Nature adopts the cloak of a flaming artist, determined to exhibit a riotous blend of pigment before surrendering

'The heavy leaf / Falls of its own will'

its offspring to the eternal protector. Exclaims poet Nozawa Boncho (1640–1714):

The heavy leaf
Falls of its own will
On this silent windless day[3]

Fall symphony: Nikko, Japan.

Autumn holds a special spot in our being; as Pico Iyer observes of his adopted home, Japan, 'it is the reddening of the maple leaves under a blaze of ceramic-blue skies that is the place's secret heart'. Perhaps it is the fragility and vulnerability of this amazing splendour that endears the season, 'that liminal space between beauty and bleakness', even more. 'Between its falling leaves and fading light, it is…an invitation to attentive stillness and absolute presence, reminding us to cherish the beauty of life not despite its perishability but precisely because of

Fall companions: Karuizawa, Japan.

Blazing finale: Karuizawa, Japan.

it; because the impermanence of things—of seasons and lifetimes and galaxies and loves—is what confers preciousness and sweetness upon them'.[4]

Music, above all, conveys the fullness of life within a limited time span. The Venetian composer Antonio Vivaldi bequeathed an immortal paean to the exhilarating, dynamic, altering rhythms of nature and our emotions in the 'Four Seasons'.[5]

The grand orchestration of seasonal change finds its counterpoint in nature's flux on a miniature scale. Here the elements indulge in playful melodies, each containing its own lyric. They come together for a moment in passionate unison, but we remain aware that the song will soon modulate in a novel key.

Temporary bond: the raindrop finds companions to shelter on a leaf for some precious moments, Balestrand, Norway.

Destination unknown, Sognefjord, Norway.

Individualist, Sognefjord, Norway.

Arrangement, Sognefjord, Norway.

Just as we learn to embrace the tides of transience, we realize the creative potential of imperfection. Leaving the door open for cracks and blemishes becomes an avenue for seeking inventive solutions. The Japanese art form kintsugi applies golden lacquer in restoring broken pieces, an amplification of the profound wabi-sabi that celebrates beauty in flaw and incompleteness.

Yomeimon Gate, Ieyasu Tokugawa shrine: Nikko, Japan.

Imperfection may carry its own potency, too. At the Yomeimon gate of the shrine for the Japanese shogun[6] Tokugawa Ieyasu, the twelve carved pillars reveal a repeated pattern resembling curved fern leaves. On one of the pillars, though, the design is upside-down, called sakasabashira. This deliberate 'mistake' prevents the gate from ever reaching a state of completion or perfection, echoing the Japanese belief that a state of perfection results in deterioration and collapse. This gate certainly embodies the magic of imperfection, having survived the tumultuous waves of history and continuing to honour the shogun who set Japan upon the path of stability and prosperity.

Sakasabashira: the upside-down pillar, Tokugawa shrine, Nikko, Japan.

Bringing ourselves in step with impermanence and imperfection, we discover that freedom comes from flowing with the changes (and flaws) in life.

Completion: a Journey in Emptiness and Release

'We have fallen into the place
where everything is music….
Open the window in the center of your chest,
and let the spirits fly in and out.'

—Rumi[1]

The brevity of our lifespan energizes the search for fulfilment, for those moments or paths that seem to illuminate the purpose

Borobudur Temple, Indonesia, on Waisak: the Buddha's birth, enlightenment, and 'parinirvana'.

of our existence. Here we can draw upon the wisdom and insights of inspired souls as we carve out our individual journeys, secure in the comfort of belonging to the bonds of humankind since the first hesitant but determined steps of wandering. Each spark of intuition and understanding pierces our core, fusing in the luminous chords of a radiant symphony.

The puzzle of existence continues to accost us at all stages of life, sparking multiple forms of distress and negative emotions. Prince Siddhartha Gautama chose to abandon his regal comforts, wandering in deprivation and intense self-inquiry to discern the balm that would

The lamp of sukha (freedom from suffering): Borobudur Temple, Indonesia.

heal suffering. As the Buddha, his path has shone the light on countless generations of grateful fellow travellers.

Among the greatest challenges confronting humans is the nature of the mind: conditioned from an early age to turn into a chattering

Release: the lightness of being, Borobudur Temple, Indonesia.

machine, fuelled by layers of craving and grasping, morphing into a formidable inner critic. The process of recovery involves a gradual silencing of the chatter and an examination of its contents. Here we find a daunting medley of conceptions, assumptions, and deep-seated biases—of birth, race, gender, ethnicity, nationality, religion, social class, education, politics—the poisoned and piercing arrows that have resulted in human conflict and destructive attitudes through the ages. No wonder the Buddha called his approach swimming against the current. His example inspired others to withstand the powerful tides and transform the mind into a calming, cooling vessel of equanimity, flowing with the heartfelt, noble impulses of non-violence and compassion.

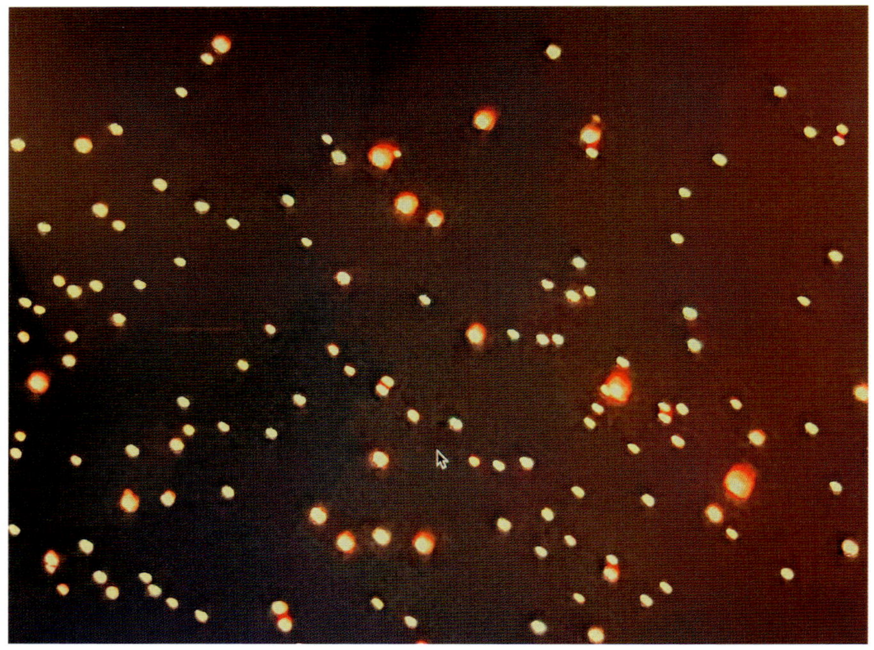

Cosmic unity, Borobudur Temple, Indonesia.

Freed from the cage of destructive notions and emotions, we move toward the dynamic state of emptiness—fresh, receptive, open to new experiences. At the Waisak ceremony in the Borobudur Temple, we follow the Buddha's uplifting story on the gracefully sculptured walls before witnessing the lighting and flight of lanterns into the night sky. As these exquisite beacons soar toward the cosmic domains, we feel a joyful expansion and the release of sorrows and burdens. Emptiness gifts us a new lightness of being.

The Harmandir Sahib in Amritsar emanates its own golden light, resonating with the sounds of generosity and brotherhood in the revered voice of Guru Nanak.[2] As the ragis[3] fill the air with melodious verses, pilgrims are imbued with Nanak's vision that the truly religious person is one who regards all humans as equals and shares his wealth with others rather than hoard it for himself. Sikhs in all corners of the globe honour Nanak's principles with warm companionship and selfless service to others without distinction. A shining example is the langar or communal kitchen which ensures that no individual goes hungry in its vicinity.

Harmandir Sahib, Golden Temple: Amritsar, India.

Similar to mystics and seers through the ages, Nanak recognized the trap of the individual self, created and fortified by social convention, bolstered with notions of pride, arrogance, and exclusion. This is the source of the limited existence, but in removing the fetters of egotism, Nanak experienced unlimited bliss and a liberated mind and heart finding communion with all forms of life.

Soaking in the tranquil radiance of the Golden Temple and the warm meal at its langar, I feel the limitless possibility of the spirit and an enduring rapport with all that exists.

Even the seeming cessation of life has never deterred humans from attempting to defy its physical finality. The souls of ancestors grace the expanse of magnificent shrines, resurrected by the curing power of remembrance. At the Shakhi Zinda[4] necropolis in Samarkand, the entwined destinies of Islam and Uzbek glory permeate the walls. The cousin of Prophet Muhammad, Qusam-ibn-Abbas, shares mausoleum space with Turkan Ago, the niece of Uzbeg hero Amir Timur, and his sister, Shirin Bika Aga. As I wander, transfixed by the sumptuous artistry of the sacred spaces, the call of the adzan (the Islamic prayer, a recitation from the Qu'ran) fills the noon air with the invitation to

The power of remembrance: Shakhi Zinda, Samarkand, Uzbekistan.

contemplate the majesty and benevolence of the Merciful One.

In the company of the departed, the past unites with the present, and we experience a renewed sense of vitality and gratitude for the precious gift bestowed upon us by the immortal supreme being.

Immortal ancestors: Shakhi Zinda, Samarkand, Uzbekistan.

Knots of devotion: Shakhi Zinda, Samarkand, Uzbekistan.

Call to prayer: Shakhi Zinda, Samarkand, Uzbekistan.

Doorway to paradise: Shakhi Zinda, Samarkand, Uzbekistan.

At some hallowed spots, the notion of past and present, of time itself, seems to disappear. Globetrotter Mark Twain mused that Varanasi, on the banks of the river Ganga, 'is older than history, older than tradition, older even than legend, and looks twice as old as all of them put together'. As a contemporary traveller makes their way through the narrow lanes, jostled by rickshaws, cows, swarms of humanity, and assaulted by scents of every conceivable kind arising from its hoary alleyways, Varanasi exudes an other-worldly aura. As the navel of an entire cosmology, 'a living text of Hinduism',[5] it appears detached from the Earth, its sacred geography placing it atop the trident of its lord and protector, Sada Shiva, the eternal. Varanasi is the unmoving witness of the human spectacle, yet also its shining inspiration, explaining the city's first and popular name, Kashi or the City of Light.

The luminosity of Varanasi radiates the genius of Hindu thought and civilization, its ability to meld multiplicity and unity in a dazzling synthesis. By some counts, 330 million deities are worshipped in diverse corners of India with an astonishing array of rituals and practices, yet they are considered emanations of one supreme principle: Brahman. For those who worship Shiva, he is the unifier of every aspect. All distinctions seem to melt away in Varanasi: pure and impure, wealth and poverty, sound and silence; in his form as Ardhanarishvara (portrayed as part god and part goddess), Shiva removes the divergence of male and female too. Ambiguities are often the lifeblood of human existence, but here they coalesce in celebration of a cosmic pulse.

As I wander down the ghats (steps leading to a river) of Varanasi, I meet a spectacle at every step. Men and women, fathers and sons, mothers and daughters celebrate what is believed to be a cleansing dip in the holy water. A girl and her mother conjure vibrant designs and colours to bring a goddess into being. A beautiful young lady poses with the river and boats as buoyant backdrop. An elderly woman cooks a meal while another prays at a shrine. Goats frolic and nibble at stray leaves, while a resting dog finds himself showered with petals from a worshipper. At the morning and evening aarti[6] (a Hindu religious ceremony including lighted lamps and hymns of devotion; literally meaning 'complete love' for the deity), young men whirl flaming torches to the accompaniment of melodic chants and the haunting timbre of conch shells. An elderly pilgrim slumbers on the pavement, carrying his entire world with him.

The river of light: Ganga, Varanasi, India.

Holy dip, Varanasi, India.

Creating the goddess: Varanasi, India.

Devotion: Varanasi, India.

Moonlight Sonata: Varanasi, India.

Every face tells a story, and here, it is a tale of serenity, unmatched and rare in our frenzied, frantic era. Perhaps that explains why many wanderers feel nearer here to the heart of the world.

Trishul shakti (the power of Lord Shiva's trident): Varanasi, India.

Renunciation: Varanasi, India.

Dissolution, completion: Varanasi, India.

At the Manikarnika and Harish Chandra ghats, stacks of wood remain prepared to turn into funeral pyres, while boats continue plying down the tranquil waters. Even the implacable opposition of life and death dissolves here. Fire is both destroyer and purifier.

For the believer, to die in Varanasi is to achieve mukti, liberation from the cycle of birth, demise, and rebirth.

We commenced with the whispers of creation and culminate in the silence of completion. In the interlude lies the wondrous journey.

Notes

INTRODUCTION

1. A term from Chinese thought and wisdom that implies the complementary nature of seeming opposites or contradictions.
2. Eknath Easwaran, *The Dhammapada*, London: Arkana, 1987, p. 71.

NATURE: A JOURNEY IN AWE AND HUMILITY

1. Jeff Pepper, Xiao Hui Wang, *Dao De Jing in Clear English*, Verona: Imagin8 Press, 2018, p. 9.
2. An Italian musical term—at a leisurely, moderate pace, akin to a stroll.
3. To complement the Arcadian landscapes of Kashmir, listen to the beguiling sounds they inspire in the 'Call of the Valley', played by the masters of the santoor (a stringed instrument, played with mallets), flute, guitar, and tabla (a kind of drums), available at <https://www.youtube.com/watch?v=yFWfF3Zow74&t=599s>.
4. Katsushika Hokusai (1760–1849) and Ando Hiroshige (1797–1858) were masters of the 'Ukiyo-e' or 'pictures of the floating world' printmaking movement in nineteenth-century Japan, known for their urban scenes and landscapes, including multiple views of Mount Fuji.
5. Yanying Lu, 'Water Metaphors in *Dao de jing*: A Conceptual Analysis', *Open Journal of Modern Linguistics*, Vol. 2, No. 4, 24 October 2012.
6. The French Impressionist composer, Claude Debussy, captured this dramatic engagement in his mesmerizing piano piece, 'La cathédrale engloutie' ('The engulfed cathedral'). When you are at leisure, hear it played by the Brazilian pianist Nelson Freire, available at <https://www.youtube.com/watch?v=cVMGwPDP-Yk>.
7. Suzanne Simard, 'How Trees Talk to Each Other', available at <https://www.youtube.com/watch?v=Un2yBgIAxYs>.
8. Listen to the recording by the Emerson String Quartet, available at <https://www.youtube.com/watch?v=6rCapLO-6eU>.
9. Hear the animated Manganiyar folk singers welcome the sprinkling of the heavens in 'Jhilmil barse megh' and marvel at the sound of castanets with echoes of the gypsy Flamenco of Spain, an indicator of the human capacity to traverse barriers and boundaries in a common flourishing, available at <https://www.youtube.com/watch?v=qsqOLezRNW4>.
10. Stewart W. Holmes, Chimyo Horioka, *Zen Art for Meditation*, Tokyo: Charles E. Tuttle Company, 1973, p. 39.
11. Osho, *Intuition: Knowing beyond Logic*, New York: St. Martin's Press, 2001, p. 177.
12. Ibid, p. 181.

THE ARTS: A JOURNEY IN WONDER AND CATHARSIS

1. Jinpa is a renowned Tibetan scholar and translator for His Holiness the Dalai Lama.
2. A visit to the Van Gogh Museum in Amsterdam brings us in thrall to the artist's stirring self-portraits, apart from multiple aspects of his genius.
3. The depictions of *The Scream* in varied media can be viewed at the Munch Museum in Oslo, Norway.
4. Lovingly tended in his garden at Giverny, water lilies became an inspiring theme for Monet's genius, moving from realistic depictions to impressions in colour and line, hinting at the source of the creative spark in nature and humans alike. We can enjoy this enthralling progression at the Musée d'Orsay and the Musée de l'Orangerie in Paris; at the Orangerie, Monet used an elliptical space to shatter the conventional boundaries of the frame and bring the artist (and the viewer) into communion with an elemental energy.
5. Listen to the galvanizing 'Eroica', appropriately played by the Vienna Philharmonic Orchestra under the baton of the legendary Leonard Bernstein, available at <https://www.youtube.com/watch?v=RkP33esCi5g>.
6. Beethoven merged orchestra and chorus in the stirring final movement of his Symphony No. 9, set to Friedrich Schiller's poem, and it has been adopted by the European Union as its anthem.
7. Haruki Murakami, *First Person Singular*, New York: Alfred A. Knopf, 2021, p. 68.
8. Khajuraho is in central India, Badami in the southern state of Karnataka. The Mughals, who ruled much of India from the sixteenth to the eighteenth century, encouraged a blend of Persian and Indian cultures and arts, including architecture, painting, music, dance, and cuisine.
9. Photo from <http://aasarchitecture.com>, last accessed on 6 June 2021.
10. After a devastating fire in 2019, the restored Notre-Dame reopened to the grateful visitor in December 2024.
11. Listen to Fatma Said and Marianne Crebassa's rendition, available at <https://www.youtube.com/watch?v=eTyxSjeSfCE>.
12. Her novel, *A Many Splendoured Thing* (Harmondsworth: Penguin Books), was published in 1952 and turned into a Hollywood film in 1955.
13. V. A. Smith, *Khajuraho Unveiled*, Greenage Books, 2010, p. 207.
14. These terms connote a well-mannered way of life, cradled in respect and politeness, which shape behaviour as well as cultural exchange.
15. 'Eating for your brain with Dr Lisa Mosconi', available at <www.youtube.com/watch?v=qxiAmJllp4I&t=1180s>.
16. This is a polyphenol or anti-oxidant, a healthy ingredient in red wine.

EXCHANGE: A JOURNEY IN ENDURANCE AND EFFLORESCENCE

1. Shan Sa, *Empress: a Novel*, New York: HarperCollins, 2006, p. 159.
2. Ibid.

3. The Hindu god of Creation (with the cosmic vibration of dance) and Destruction (particularly of ignorance and evil).
4. Located close to Yogyakarta in central Java, the Borobudur was built by the Syailendra dynasty in the eighth and ninth centuries CE, a monument to the exchange of cultural ideas and influences between India and Indonesia.
5. Traditional Islamic ruler, but the sultans of Yogyakarta preserved the syncretic blend of practices from multiple cultures and beliefs, encapsulated in Kejawèn, or the Javanese way of life, which played a prominent role in shaping modern Indonesia after its independence in 1945.
6. Peter Suwarno, *Dictionary of Javanese Proverbs and Idiomatic Expressions*, Yogyakarta: Gadjah Mada University Press, 1999, p. 34.

SEPARATION AND LOSS: A JOURNEY IN SOLITUDE AND RESILIENCE

1. Yuki Sawa, Edith Marcombe Shiffert, *Haiku Master Buson: Translations from the Writings of Yosa Buson—Poet and Artist—with Related Materials*, Buffalo: White Pine Press, 2007.
2. Stephen Batchelor, *The Art of Solitude*, New Haven: Yale University Press, 2020.
3. Ibid.
4. Lama Alan Wallace on Wisdom Dharma Chats, available at <https://wisdomexperience.org/dharma-chats/>.

IMPERMANENCE: A JOURNEY IN FLUIDITY AND TRANSIENCE

1. Perhaps none has captured this captivating display better than the Russian composer Tchaikovsky in his 'Waltz of the Snowflakes' from my favourite ballet, 'The Nutcracker', available at <https://www.youtube.com/watch?v=fLKhWl3tEkk>.
2. Stewart W. Holmes, Chimyo Horioka, *Zen Art for Meditation*, Tokyo: Charles E. Tuttle Company, 1973, p. 85.
3. Ibid, p. 111.
4. Maria Popova, 'Autumn Light: Pico Iyer on Finding Beauty in Impermanence and Luminosity in Loss', *The Marginalian*, available at <https://www.themarginalian.org/2019/10/11/autumn-light-pico-iyer/>.
5. Hear the zestful version by Dmitry Sinkovsky and La Voce Strumentale, available at <https://www.youtube.com/watch?v=YmYq0lQOt1A&t=231s>.
6. Shoguns were military leaders in Japan and the de-facto rulers for long periods of time, although the emperor remained the symbolic ruler. The Tokugawa clan ruled Japan from 1603 to 1867, providing the foundations for economic growth and cultural flourishing before the restoration of the Meiji emperor in 1868.

COMPLETION: A JOURNEY IN EMPTINESS AND RELEASE

1. Coleman Barks (tr.), *Like This / Rumi*, Athens(GA):Maypop, 1990, p. 48.
2. The founder of the Sikh faith, lived from 1469 to 1539.

3. Singers of devotional hymns or Gurbani kirtan.
4. Literally, 'the living king'.
5. Diana L. Eck, *Banaras: City of Light*, Princeton: Princeton University Press, 1982, p. 9.
6. Experience the vibrating pulsation of the aarti available at <https://www.youtube.com/watch?v=kegsMwaH63E>.